I cope

Cover Illustration by *Mallory Whitten*
CCM Design & Cover *Michael J Seidlinger*
ISBN - 978-1-937865-31-3

For more information, find CCM at:

http://copingmechanisms.net

IF I REALLY WANTED TO FEEL HAPPY I'D FEEL HAPPY ALREADY

jordan castro

~~contents~~

haiku
baker three
philosophy poem

~~self-help: life-affirming~~
~~philosophy rooted in~~
~~existentialism,~~
~~cognitive-behavioral~~
~~therapy,~~
~~and the unidirectional~~
~~nature of time~~

the secret is that you are enough

through a calm, detached, mildly ambitious perception and assessment of situations and circumstances

i can increase intelligence levels, power levels, and good feelings in my brain

through the ingestion of mostly raw organic vegan foods and the appropriate movement of my muscles

i can increase lifespan, physiological health, and well-being in general

this is important to me because i am not currently in the act of committing immediate suicide

i am perpetuating the idea that life is desirable during every moment in which i am existing in a state of 'not earnestly trying to kill myself immediately'

every sentient being who is currently existing in a state of 'not earnestly trying to kill myself immediately' is displaying an interest in being alive

*

thoughts control emotions and behaviors

this means that in order to feel good or act in a desirable manner, one must process thoughts in a way that effectively enables this emotional/behavioral response

*

'you don't owe anything to anyone, because each moment is it's own moment, separate from all other moments' and 'you are not you in past moments, you are you now, always' allow for easy cognitive adjustments and modifications

resulting in emotional/behavioral adjustments and modifications resulting in a state of being that can embrace change, inconsistency, and death

*

'pursuit of ownership over anything besides yourself' is counterproductive—nothing can ever be yours besides you

and the secret is that you are enough

~~stupid~~

feels like i'm just getting dumber as life goes on
like just getting pretty dumb or whatever

*

i can feel a dense disconnection from writing a poem

as a goal-oriented organism

who feels extremely depressed and incapable

of accomplishing the goal

of writing a poem

*

i can feel an even denser disconnection from myself

as a goal-oriented organism

due to acute feelings of extreme depression, anxiety, and inadequacy

that are (in)directly derived from my dense disconnection from

writing a poem

to express my feelings of extreme depression, anxiety, and inadequacy

*

i can feel an unbelievably dense disconnection from you

typing ‘i love you’

into gmail chat

two hundred and forty-five miles away

due to my dense disconnection from myself

as a goal-oriented organism

and my feelings of extreme depression, anxiety, and
inadequacy

that are (in)directly derived from my dense disconnection from

writing a poem

about myself

haiku

i wish we were near
each other so i could hold
your hand and kiss you

~~cute~~

i say ‘whend are you going to cumb ober?’

you say ‘i think...maybe ind fifteend mindits?’

i say ‘otayb. i will see you thend’

*

i press down hard while petting your head

you make a face and say for me to stop it

you grab my arm and hold it away from your head

i repeatedly attempt to pet you

you grab my arm and wiggle your body

you say for me to stop it

*

you answer your phone in an excited tone of voice

i feel happy and surprised

*

driving at night

my right arm is around you and your head is on my chest

we listen to music at a low volume and sing along gently

haiku

looking at your face
thinking unrelated thoughts
'my poetry file'

~~at school people say things~~

i can feel myself turn inward

the escalation from ‘politely responding with terse expressions of acknowledgment’

to

‘feeling my face morph into something soft and wet while seconds turn to minutes turn to hours turn to years and i am staring and nodding and smiling strangely and maybe saying “yeah” or “uh huh” while internally moving at a speed of one hundred miles per hour and experiencing feelings in a linear manner that go from anxiety to self-hatred to self-aware self-hatred to sarcastic self-aware self-hatred to “what is going on” to “what...” to thoughts about myself in terms of the current social situation to thoughts about myself in terms of some insanely large context like forever to thoughts about myself in terms of myself to extreme feelings of detachment to nothing while having already started to feel even more anxiety about the prospect of tweeting said feeling, which is really many feelings, a poly-feeling, which may or may not be explicable in 140 characters or less in a manner that is clear, enjoyable, and relatable’

happens quickly

my face feels numb and my mouth, i think, is open

someone smiles at me

i fall further into myself, screaming

~~head cold~~

i honestly feel like i am drowning!

suffocating!

flailing my arms and thrashing about!

i feel depressed!

but like a retarded infant feeling depressed!

who feels sarcastic about being a retarded infant!

feeling depressed!

with a head cold!

i can no longer function!

took four nyquil!

still can't sleep!

thoughts keep coming!

'he tossed and turned. he thought about school!'

'i feel so...suicide is imminent...can i tweet this shit...this...shit...
this...shit...!'

entering my head like they're from somewhere, someone else!

and my head feels like an enlarged version of my head as an
infant!

pixilated and gigantic!

my face feels full of phlegm!

i can't do anything!

i am trapped inside this body!

my face will always be my face!

no matter what!

unless i get a face transplant, which someone has actually done!

my heart will always be my heart!

no matter what!

fucked!

tortured!

i want xanax!

i can't do anything about this head cold!

i should just accept it!

and move on!

but i'm not!

i feel insane!

what is happening!

whas hannin!

i can't stop thinking!

i want to take drugs!

my phone is ringing!

i know it's mallory!

i just thought 'gahhh' in a manner like i was a fire-breathing dragon who was stabbed in the side by a knight!

and the knight was a head cold!

and i want to fucking kill myself!

everything's so bad!

tomorrow is friday!

i want to take drugs at night, walk around a city!

i want to be productive, work on things!

i feel like i am slowly descending into a river!

water rushing into my skull!

dying!

slowly!

painfully!

retarded pizza infant!

~~at any given moment~~
~~i will shrink~~

the goal is a sponge that never dries

i will shrink into something the size of a fingernail

ugly, alien, afraid

yesterday at the library a man sat next to me

i left immediately

the goal is a complex-tasting health food that is organic and filling

'nom nom'

when i shrink, you will watch helplessly, wishing something had happened differently, but

nothing can ever happen differently than it has already happened

and the goal is simple

small

~~we, waiting, want~~

i feel strange and upset when you say bad things about other people

he said she said we said we

are waiting for something to take us somewhere far away

somewhere better

but there isn't anywhere better to go

the difference between 'want' and 'think we want' is fundamental and tragic

murder or be murdered. my facial expression is blank

at school, people seem insane

'sitting in my room, what should i do'

wait

~~goals~~

my life goal is to reach a state of 'steady monetary income for minimal amount of work that i don't want to do'

long term

some of my short term goals include 'utilizing my "free time" to promote my literary career' and 'eating a "giant fucking salad" sometime soon, because i'm hungry'

food is a physiological necessity intrinsic in all animals

and governments, republicans, democrats, meat-eaters, the USDA, and police are (in)directly making it insanely hard for certain demographics of people and other animals to obtain food

every six seconds a human child under the age of twelve dies of starvation

seconds are unidirectional and age is a preconceived notion based on time (which is unidirectional) - meaning age does not represent wisdom or seniority, it just denotes itself, whatever that is

some of my other life goals include 'feeling like i recently ingested coffee without having recently ingested coffee' and 'making the world a better place for people who are "born into shit"'

a person who is born does not decide to be born

things just happen this way

a person does not ask to pick coffee beans for two cents an hour, to pay for food, to feed their children and themselves, to maintain internal body heat, to remain breathing, etc

a person does not ask for this

things just happen this way

other life goals of mine include 'acceptance' and 'the complete realization of the thought that "things just happen this way"'

i want to treat my body and my brain well and sensually experience/ingest only that which will aid me in obtaining my goals

i want to use my thoughts to control my emotions and behaviors, because thoughts control emotions and behaviors and thoughts are perceptions of everything we experience sensually

and because i want to feel productive and satisfied, physiologically and cognitively

okay

ancestors

i left school during third period
i drove my car on I-480 west toward your house
i smoked cigarettes and listened to music at a high volume
through speakers

when i got there you were eating tofu scramble and toast

you said have you seen this show before
i said no what is it
you said it's always sunny in philadelphia
you said it's really funny

i looked at the TV

i said this is really funny

i said do you have a tuner
you said no

i tuned my guitar to the low e string of my guitar
you tuned your banjo to my guitar

we played songs together

we drank coffee

we smoked cigarettes on your deck
we listened to your friend interview good old war on the radio

i put my arm around you in a 'buddy buddy' way

i drove home
i thought about some things
i didn't listen to music

~~the last time you called~~

you said are you happy

you said remember when you and ziggy used to drink arizona green tea before school

you said the georgia peach kind

you said remember when you called me like three days after you turned vegan and you had pizza in your hand

you said my new boyfriend is good at sex

you said twice

you said in a car

you said remember when you used to laugh so hard

you said i can imagine it

you said do you remember

~~haiku~~

staring at paper
trying to think of something
forgot what it was

~~in the heights~~

we went to a play
i saw a male and a female grab each others butts
i said he just grabbed her ass
you expressed confusion
i noticed the ass grabbers were people from our school
we sat down
my brother wanted to sit next to my dad
i sat in the seat closest to the aisle
the play started
the play was about poor people from the dominican republic
who were trying to overcome their
    situations but couldn't seem to overcome them
we shared a box of sour patch kids
there was rapping
we switched seats
i said i have to pee so bad but there's a huge line
we walked to the upper part of the theatre
we walked to another theatre that was connected to the theatre
we were in but a man said we
    couldn't enter if we didn't have tickets
we walked to the bathroom
i waited in line
a man said i hired my 150th employee a few days ago
a man said god bless you
i peed
i washed my hands
i walked out of the bathroom
we talked
we walked to our seats
some girls from my choir class sat in front of us
we said things about the girls from my choir class
the play ended
my parents drove us to my house
i put some things into a backpack
i told my mom i was sleeping at evan's house
i drove to your house
i smoked a nat sherman brand cigarette in my car
we walked into your house

i looked for allergy medicine in cupboards
i looked for allergy medicine in my car
i swallowed two claritin
we made a video of ourselves mixing coca-cola with disaronno brand liquor while listening to ‘o
let’s do it’ by waka flocka flam
we drank coca-cola with disaronno brand liquor
we said things about school
i signed into gmail
we video chatted with david
i gmail chatted with tao
we told david that we would video chat with him later
we gmail chatted with tao
i drank a 24 ounce can of coors banquet brand beer
tao said that he was trying on clothes for a plane ride to taiwan
we laughed a lot
we video chatted with david
i walked into your garage
i smoked three-fourths of a nat sherman brand cigarette
i walked inside
i signed out of gmail
we walked upstairs
we lied in your bed
we held each other
you said i want to give you a blowjob but it might be too loud
i said i am drunk and tired and it might be too loud
we kissed
we fell asleep
i woke up
you said i made you breakfast
you ate oatmeal
i fell asleep
i woke up
i said hi to your mom
we lied in bed
we talked
your mom left
i got dressed
i called my dad
i walked into the bathroom

i sat on the toilet
i pooped
i reached for toilet paper
i stood up while leaning forward and holding my shirt away from my butt
i looked in cupboards for toilet paper
i looked at the trash can
i touched things in the trash can
i called your cell phone three times
i sent text messages to david
i yelled something
i said there is no toilet paper
you said the door is locked
i stood up
i unlocked the door
i sat down
you threw toilet paper to me
i caught the toilet paper
i wiped my butt
i walked downstairs
i drank a cup of coffee
we talked
we kissed
i left

~~vegan~~

at school someone said

so...what do you eat?

i said i don't know, like, i actually eat mostly normal foods i guess

felt terrible

~~unable to make~~
~~fundamental decisions~~

last night i typed ‘i feel tht my arms are a sepratt part of ym body’

due to lifetimes of conflicting experiences, my parents will never be able to interpret my behavior with an earnest sense of empathy or understanding, making it impossible for us to ever know each other beyond our innate roles as parent/child

i don’t know what i’m talking about

last night was sunday night

this morning i put on clothes

twenty minutes later i ran upstairs and changed them

i want to bury my face in one thousand pillows and cry when i think of your name

i want my facial hair to latch onto your face when we kiss

i want to whimper quietly in the face of imminent danger

this morning i stood in my kitchen for over five minutes trying to decide whether or not to put organic dried cranberries on my salad because of the unnecessary consumption of resources and calories versus added flavor

~~positive~~

at school someone said

are you still in a band?

i said i mean, like, sort of...like, we still play together a little, but we're not like, serious or whatever

felt terrible

~~the cyclical, binary nature of thoughts and emotions~~

i feel strongly the possibility that i will never feel any other way
than the way i'm feeling now

every time i feel something

which may or may not mean i feel that all the time

i understand too that this is not true

which can cause me to feel happy

sad or indifferent

depending on the initial feeling

and my level of awareness of other feelings

which evolved from other feelings

so invariably

i feel differently than the way i felt before

etc

*

if anybody else has repeatedly thought things like ‘i hate my life,’ ‘i want to die,’ and/or ‘fuck all you bitches’ while at the same time feeling incredibly motivated to achieve myriad personal goals that are probably rooted in the feelings derived from the external validation that the accomplishment of said goals will bring you

please e-mail me

jordancastroisthepresident@gmail.com

~~the last, and~~

Sarah and Lilly are driving. Sarah sees a black man walking on the sidewalk. "Sup black," Sarah says to Lilly. Lilly smiles.

The girls stop at a red light next to a teenage boy who is alone. He is moving his head and singing very loudly. "Roll down your window and try to get his attention," says Sarah. Lilly rolls down her window and waves her arms. The boy looks at the girls and slowly rolls down his window.

"Hey faggot," Sarah says.

"Say it louder," Lilly says.

"We are at a red light," Sarah says. "It'd be weird."

"My friend says she wants to give you a blowjob," Lilly says to the boy.

"I didn't say that," Sarah says to the boy. "I didn't," she mumbles.

The light is green. The boy rolls up his window and quickly drives away.

Sarah feels tired. She is having a sleepover with two of her friends. She is using her laptop. One of her friends is playing an unplugged electric guitar. Her other friend is lying on the ground. Sarah opens the Gmail draft of her novella. She types the words, 'Jessica Alba is a dumb bitch.' She grins. She deletes the words. She says "What do you guys want to do, it's midnight."

"Can I smoke a cigarette on your roof," one of her friends says.

"Yeah," Sarah says. "Be quiet though."

Sarah's friend struggles to open the window. She opens the window. She climbs out of the window and onto the roof. Sarah feels a breeze.

Two days later Sarah is sitting inside of a coffee shop. It is nine o'clock p.m. Her friend is having a release show for his environmental awareness zine. There are people singing loudly. Sarah is looking at her laptop and typing words to Liz on Gmail chat.

"There are people freaking out in this coffee shop," Sarah types.

"Damn," Liz types.

Sarah stares at the screen. She has never met Liz in real life.

"I want to meet a cute boy," Sarah types. "Like a really cute indie boy or something."

"Hehe," Liz types. "Seems like I feel too tired to meet new people. Like going through the necessary motions seems impossible."

"Damn," Sarah types. "I honestly feel like all relationships are really systematic, maybe."

"Totally bro," Liz types. "Totes magotes, bro."

"Hehe," Sarah types. "Damn."

"Like, I feel like in order to meet a cute guy, you just have to like, meet them, start talking slightly, get their number, text them sometimes, mostly seem cool and sexy but also seem busy, and then move in for the kill. It honestly seems that simple to me," Liz types.

"Damn," Sarah types.

"Damn," Liz types. "Seems depressing."

"I don't know," Sarah types.

"I don't know," Liz types. "I'm gonna go. Gonna walk around the city."

"Okay," Sarah types. "Bye."

Later, Sarah is staring at the home page of her blog. She is feeling anxiety about how many people have left comments on her most recent post. She is typing words to people on Gmail chat. She stares blankly with unfocused eyes at the corner of her laptop. 'What am I doing,' she thinks. 'What can I do to feel better right now.' She closes her laptop and looks around the room. She opens her laptop and looks at Gmail. She looks at her blog. She closes her laptop. She lies down on her bed.

Five nights later Sarah is staring at the home page of her blog. She opens a new tab and types www.twitter.com. She sees that someone RT'd a tweet about her most recently released e-book. The person is from Germany. Sarah clicks on Gmail. She Gmail chats with someone. She types 'gtg.' She changes her status to 'invisible.' She looks at her blog. She looks at Twitter. She looks at her blog. She closes her laptop. She sleeps.

Sarah wakes up 14 hours later. She opens her laptop. She lies in bed and stares at the screen. She looks at Gmail, Blogger, Statcounter, Twitter, YouTube, Myspace, Flickr, and Last F.M. She clicks on YouTube and types 'Lil Wayne Freestyle' into the search bar. She clicks the third option. She thinks 'I have seen this before.' She watches half of the video and clicks the second option in the 'Related Videos' section on the right side of the screen. The video is called 'Pill Poppin Animal.' She types 'Beirut' into the search bar and clicks the second option. She sings along to the video quietly. She stops singing. She walks to the bathroom. She pees. She brushes her teeth. She washes her hands. She washes her face. She looks in the mirror. She thinks 'It is freezing.'

John K. Samson is singing a song on YouTube. It is 5:36 a.m. Sarah is crying into her hands. John K. Samson sings Like the jokes about my figure kids think I don't understand, I know I'm just your little ampersand. Sarah is invisible on Gmail chat and no one appears to be online. Sarah tries to Gmail chat Liz, even though it says that Liz is offline. Sarah does not get a response. Just your little ampersand. Sarah stops crying. She walks to the bathroom. She poops. She reads two paragraphs of "Less Than Zero." She walks out of the bathroom. She closes her laptop. She sleeps.

The next day, Sarah is at school. She walks to Trigonometry class. She walks to Drawing class. She walks to Chemistry class. She walks to English class. She walks to lunch. She sits next to Peter. Sarah eats batter dipped tofu, spinach, pita chips, and hummus. Peter eats strawberries, a peanut butter sandwich, and nuts.

"How are you," Peter says.

"Okay," Sarah says. "How are you?"

"Not bad," Peter says.

The lunchroom is crowded. People are talking loudly. Peter puts his hand on Sarah's back.

Peter puts his hand into his backpack and takes out a banana. "F yeah," he says.

Sarah smiles. "Awesome," she says.

One month later Sarah's cell phone alarm buzzes at 6:05AM. She presses the 'snooze' button. Sarah's cell phone alarm buzzes at 6:10AM. She presses the 'snooze' button. Sarah's cell phone alarm buzzes at 6:15AM. She presses the 'snooze' button. Sarah's cell phone alarm buzzes at 6:20AM. She presses the 'snooze' button. Sarah's cell phone alarm buzzes at 6:25AM. She presses the 'dismiss' button. She gets out of bed.

Sarah walks into the bathroom. She brushes her teeth. She showers for thirteen minutes. She dries herself with a towel. She poops. She notices that her butt cheeks feel damp. She wipes. She sits on her bed to dry her butt cheeks. She moves her legs in a circular motion. She rolls onto her back. She puts on a button up shirt from American Apparel, a tie from H&M, a sweater vest from H&M, jeans from Old Navy, Puma brand socks, and a hoody from Old Navy. She walks downstairs.

Sarah puts a salad, an organic apple, Stacy's brand pita chips, and hummus into her backpack. She brews coffee and pours the coffee into a thermos. She puts on shoes. She walks out the door. She drives. She listens to The Mountain Goats, WHY?, and Sam Cooke. She arrives at school twenty minutes before first period starts. She sits down against a locker next to Peter.

"Morning," Peter says.

"Morning," Sarah says. Peter holds out his hand for Sarah to touch. Sarah thinks, 'He always wants some of my coffee.' She hands him her coffee. Peter takes a sip of the coffee.

Sarah walks to Trigonometry class. She walks to Drawing class. She walks to Chemistry class. She walks to English class. She walks to lunch. She walks to Choir class. She walks to Journalism class. She walks to Psychology class. She walks to her car. She drives home.

At home, Sarah opens her laptop. She looks at Gmail, Blogger, Statcounter, Twitter, Goodreads, YouTube, and Last F.M. She eats a banana. She drives to work.

At work, Sarah delivers pizza, folds boxes, stocks the refrigerator, makes two salads, and sweeps the floor.

Sarah arrives home at 10:03PM. She walks to her bedroom. She opens her laptop and looks at Gmail, Blogger, Statcounter, Twitter, Goodreads, and YouTube. She opens Microsoft Word.

She types 'physiological lassitude.' She deletes 'physiological lassitude' and types 'so tired.' She deletes 'so tired.' She closes her laptop and turns off the lights.

Two days later, Sarah is drinking coffee at Organic Energy. She sees a very cute hipster-looking male eating what appears to be steamed tofu and spinach. He is drinking a pink-colored smoothie. Sarah thinks 'Peter.' Sarah realizes that she has been staring at the hipster for a period of time and that the hipster has noticed. Sarah tries to sip her coffee while appearing unaffected. She spills coffee onto her shirt. She sits there for fifteen seconds. She thinks things rapidly and considers licking the coffee off of her shirt. She wipes the coffee off of her shirt using napkins. She looks at the hipster. He appears to be calm. Sarah thinks about sex. She thinks about the hipster licking her vagina. She begins to feel anxious. She thinks about going to the bathroom to masturbate. She picks up her coffee. She leaves.

The next night Sarah is in the kitchen with Peter. Peter puts spaghetti noodles into boiling water. Sarah pours Italian dressing and soy sauce into a skillet. She cuts tofu into small squares and puts the squares into the skillet. She moves the squares of tofu with tongs. Rilo Kiley is playing on her laptop through the speakers. Peter is smiling. Sarah hugs Peter. Peter moves to the rhythm of the music. He walks to the oven. He looks at eggplant. He touches the laptop.

"Who is this," Sarah says.

"Endless Mike and the Beagle Club," Peter says.

Sarah puts spinach into the skillet containing tofu. She moves the tongs. Peter puts the spaghetti into a strainer. He puts the spaghetti into a bowl. He puts Newman's brand marinara sauce into the bowl. He puts the bowl into the microwave. Sarah removes the eggplant from the oven. She puts the tofu and spinach into the bowl containing the spaghetti and marinara sauce.

"Do you want to eat now," Sarah says.

"I am hungry," Peter says.

~~life is full of possibilities~~

really drunk

listening to dntel

seems so good

~~allergic~~

got a lot of allergies

been thinking about literature

for maybe five hours

&&&

we exist inside of an incomprehensively large [something] of
nothingness. shape-shifting
nothingness.

nothingness in the form of nothingness. cyclical
nothingness.

an incomprehensively small [nothing] inside of an
amazingly gigantic nothingness. nothingness
nothingness.

perception is an illusion made possible by the
invention of 'beginning' and
'end'

nothingness, like nothingness, is [something (nothing)].

nothingness as depression, as sorrow, as sadness,
as joy

nothingness in the form of a limp penis in jeans

our perception of external reality (necessarily subjective) exists
in a never-ending war against
nothingness

play-doh nothingness. lego nothingness.

blankets of nothingness

~~take pills~~

everything i think, say, and do can be traced back to feelings of extreme inadequacy, narcissism, and 'i want to be lying in bed with you'

this week i felt insanely depressed

depression is the result of a negative thought process, a lack of serotonin, or a mixture of both

it is wednesday night

drinking jack daniel's brand whiskey

feeling extremely concerned about my physical appearance

when i'm not immersed in an adequate amount of distractions i think about food and suicide in a manner like my only hope for feeling better is the 'last ditch effort' of binge eating or killing myself

just typed some sentences about love and it's relation to power

or something

i have no idea what i am doing or believe

my parents are going out to dinner on friday

i feel depressed

if i really wanted to feel happy i would feel happy already

there are insanely depraved monster-clowns inside of my brain with insanely sharp claws

out-of-control feelings of extreme inadequacy all the time no matter what

just imagined 'out-of-control feelings of extreme inadequacy all the time no matter what' as a batman costume that i was 'slipping into' before trick-or-treating alone

i feel incredibly sad

for no concrete reason at all

i want to kill my teachers

i want to kill every politician, c.e.o, principal, and police officer

i want everybody to know what it means to live freely

and i want it now

i want it now

i want it now
i want it now

i want it now
i want it now

i want it now

i want it now
i want it now
i want it now
i want it now
i want it now
i want it now

i didn't copy and paste any of that

i am an insane bitch

extreme feelings of sympathy, empathy, idealism, and 'the messiah complex' have turned me into a depressed piece of shit who cares only for the quality of his clothes, his food, his time spent while dying

i feel positively toward maybe three people consistently, six to nine people semi-regularly, and ten to one billion people as potential book buyers, supporters, and/or fans

jesus...

not going to post this anywhere

'for myself'

i don't care about how many comments this is going to receive

just thought about posting this

and felt worried about how many comments this would receive or not receive

i feel retarded

i want a lot of caffiene

i want it now

when i told you 'xvideos.com' was on my most visited page because i was 'fucking with evan while he was sleeping,' i lied

i watch porn sometimes

at night

when i'm feeling depressed

i rarely masturbate while watching

i just watch and feel sad

i just watch with a limp penis and feel sad

i want to be sexually 'open' and fulfill [something re sex] to it's
maximum level of [something]

mentally and physically

or something

i like receiving blowjobs

i just want to feel happy

a life rooted in sustainability, rational thinking, and calm feelings

i want a lot of coffee
i want to drink like five or six or twelve cups of coffee tomorrow

this poem feels trivial and redundant

being alive feels trivial and redundant

i want to get drunk

on friday night

i don't know

i want to be sitting in my room feeling good

eating salads
doing push ups and sit ups

with plans

to move somewhere far away—an area secluded, to some
degree, with someone quiet and nice, in an apartment with
organic vegan food and a bed—drink kombucha, feel really

good

i don’t know

aol instant messenger
circa 2007

you said i am not doing anything

you said can you come over

i said can we do it

i said haha

you said shut up ;)

you said lol

i said i’m serious

i said haha

~~don't know how to fix what my life has become (gmail chat circa 2009)~~

you said i'm just dumb because i'm lazy

you said i don't want to finish thoughts

you said i don't know

i said same

i said i feel like i can't finish thoughts or something

i said i actually feel like i might be really intelligent somewhere inside of me but like it was lost a long time ago

i said i mean it's not stupidity but you know like whatever

~~serious emotional literature~~

i don't know what to type to describe my feelings of extreme detachment from reality other than

'i feel extremely detached from reality'

~~seeing my study hall~~
~~teacher sip coffee~~
~~today caused me to~~
~~imagine her sucking~~
~~a penis~~

i want to binge eat on inorganic carbohydrates and kill myself

feeling really sad about

~~[thought]~~

my sadness is a bright pink blanket, wrapped around my head

    'look at me, i'm so depressed'

new levels of self-awareness

    'just thought [thought]'

freaking out insanely

with a calm demeanor

does anyone want to give me like five thousand dollars
so i can self-publish a non-fiction book about
all my favorite rappers

attempting to cure depression

i will transform into a gigantic, efficient,

cool-looking

insanely depressed freak with a calm demeanor and a self-aware blanket

~~a certain kind of sink~~

i miss having a certain kind of sink

or a certain kind of faucet, rather

i miss having the kind of faucet i had in the bathroom at my parents' old house

haiku

coffee makes me feel
positively about things
like going to school

~~haiku~~

i don’t get enough
external validation
on the internet

baker 3

enormous discrepancies exist between things in my brain
like enormous discrepancies existing between things in my brain

when i touch my face i don't think 'i want to touch my face. i am going to touch my face now'

enormous discrepancies exist between things in my brain

i want to ollie over them

~~philosophy poem~~

i understand events as external circumstances happening to me in a linear manner consecutively for a period of time until they cease

i understand life as a series of events

i understand thoughts as subjective perceptions of concrete reality, illusions created by everything one has experienced sensually since birth

i understand emotions as abstractions created by thoughts—feeling sad, for example, would be impossible if one did not first understand the concept of 'sad' as an emotional reaction to an external circumstance—it is in this way that, if one believes s/he is able to effectively control his or her thoughts, s/he is able to control his or her emotional reaction to external circumstances

i understand actions as the way in which one chooses or allows his or her thoughts and emotions to 'manifest' or 'transform' from abstraction to [tangible thing] that directly affects concrete reality (in)directly affecting every sentient being currently existing in concrete reality, due to cause and effect

i understand cause and effect as an omnipresent force, a law of physics which states: every action committed by a sentient being on planet earth affects every other sentient being on planet earth, to varying, unknowable degrees, in an endless self-perpetuating cycle of one action into another

i understand organic iced coffee as something aiding me in my ability to write this poem and achieve desirable levels of calm, ambition, and focus

i understand money as an abstraction created by other abstractions that, given my arbitrarily defined context and goals, is 'harmful' to the human race, via 'abstractly dictating,' to some degree, ones ability to obtain needs and wants via 'forcing' certain abstractions to affect physical reality in a manner that makes said abstractions 'real'

i understand two dollars and twenty-five cents as a unit of money, as well as my means of obtaining organic iced coffee, which i am drinking now, and which, due to cause and effect, is causing certain people 'harm,' given my arbitrarily defined contexts and goals, via perpetuating the monetary system and not allowing, or 'abstractly dictating,' to some degree, said peoples' (in)ability to obtain certain needs and wants

i understand the word arbitrary as meaning 'subject to individual will or judgment without restriction,' via dictionary.com

i understand 'subject to individual will or judgment without restriction' as an objective truth that can be applied to all externalities—as nothing holds inherent value or [any abstraction]—and i also understand that this does not mean that one cannot/'should not' 'place' value or [any abstraction] on or into things, and that this does not mean that all things, or life, is 'inherently meaningless,' but that all things, or life, is 'inherently [nothing]'

i understand meaninglessness as a lack of meaning, meaning for 'meaninglessness' to exist, 'meaning' must also exist, as one abstraction could not logically exist without the other, and it is in this way that life is not 'inherently meaningless,' but that life is 'inherently [nothing],' or '[nothing] [nothing],' rather

i understand nothing as everything and everything as nothing

i understand poetry, in the context of everything and nothing, as the same thing as anything else—cheeseburgers, for example, v-neck t-shirts

i understand words as 'a unit of language, consisting of one or more spoken sounds or their written representation, that functions as a principal carrier of meaning,' via dictionary.com

i understand anything, in the context of everything and nothing, as the same as anything else

i understand everything within my arbitrarily defined context and goals in terms of other things within my arbitrarily defined context and goals

i understand this poem as something with a beginning and an ending, as everything else with a beginning and an ending, as nothing

so it has to end somehow, or something, i guess

for now

CPSIA information can be obtained at www.ICGtesting.com
Printed in the USA
LVOW11s0328260814

400941LV00003B/172/P

9 781937 865313